american
MUSIC MILESTONES

AMERICAN ROCK

GUITAR HEROES, PUNKS, AND METALHEADS

ERIK FARSETH

TWENTY-FIRST CENTURY BOOKS
MINNEAPOLIS

NOTE TO READERS: some songs and music videos by artists discussed in this book contain language and images that readers may consider offensive.

Twenty-First Century Books
A division of Lerner Publishing Group, Inc.
241 First Avenue North
Minneapolis, MN 55401 U.S.A.

Website address: www.lernerbooks.com

Library of Congress Cataloging-in-Publication Data

Farseth, Erik.
    American rock: guitar heroes, punks, and metalheads / by Erik Farseth.
        p.   cm. — (American music milestones)
    Includes bibliographical references and index.
    ISBN 978-0-7613-4503-9 (lib. bdg. : alk. paper)
    1. Rock music—United States—History and criticism—Juvenile literature.
    I. Title. II. Title: Rock and roll/alternative.
    ML3534.F39 2013
    781.660973—dc23   2011045638

Manufactured in the United States of America
1 — CG — 7/15/12

CONTENTS

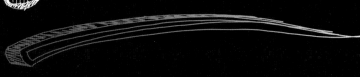

1 In The Beginning

ELVIS PRESLEY SMILED AND SLICKED BACK HIS HAIR AS HE PREPARED TO GO LIVE ON *THE ED SULLIVAN SHOW.*

The year was 1956, and Ed Sullivan was the host of the most popular television program in the United States. Sullivan had vowed that the controversial Presley would never appear on the program. But he was so popular that Sullivan changed his mind. By 1956 Presley had sold more than four million records.

Presley came out wearing a checkered jacket and clutching an acoustic guitar. He thanked the host and wiped the sweat off his brow. Bill Black started thumping the opening notes of "Don't Be Cruel" on his upright bass. Presley's backup singers leaned in toward the microphone, and he began to shake his hips. Girls in the audience screamed hysterically.

The next day, newspapers criticized Ed Sullivan for showing Elvis Presley's dancing on television. Reviewers said that Presley couldn't sing and that his music was trash. The next time that Presley performed on *The Ed Sullivan Show,* cameras only filmed him from the waist up. His legs and hips were hidden, so as not to offend older viewers. But it didn't matter—rock 'n' roll had broken through.

Elvis Presley swings his hips during a 1957 appearance on **The Ed Sullivan Show.**

THE BIRTH OF ROCK

Popular music changed forever in 1951. That year country singer Bill Haley and his band recorded "Rocket 88"—arguably the first rock 'n' roll record. A rhythm-and-blues take on "Rocket 88" had been recorded earlier that year by a group of African American musicians known as Jackie Brenston and his Delta Cats. The Delta Cats' version was a hit with R & B fans. Haley borrowed from the Delta Cats' song but added his own country style.

People had been listening to blues music for decades before rock music arrived. In the 1940s and the 1950s, white country singers and African American blues musicians started performing each other's music. The songs of Bill Haley and Elvis Presley mixed country, gospel (blues-based Christian music), and R & B. This was rock 'n' roll.

AN AXE TO GRIND

Rock music would not have been possible without the electric guitar. Electric amplification allows listeners to hear guitar players and bassists over the sound of the drums. Musicians had been using electric pickups to amplify their acoustic (nonelectric) guitars since the 1930s. But the hollow-bodied guitars they used gave off harsh feedback (noise from amplifiers). If a guitarist turned the volume up too high, his or her guitar would start to squeal. The solution was to build an electric guitar out of solid, not hollow, wood.

In 1940 the musician Les Paul created a primitive electric guitar he called the Log. The Log was made from a solid chunk of pinewood. Paul tried to sell his invention to the Gibson Guitar Corporation, but Gibson wasn't interested. Later that decade, Fender Musical Instruments developed another early electric guitar. The company's founder, Leo Fender, wasn't a musician. He couldn't even play guitar. But Fender knew to make his guitar durable and cheap for working musicians. The first Fender Telecaster hit shelves in 1951.

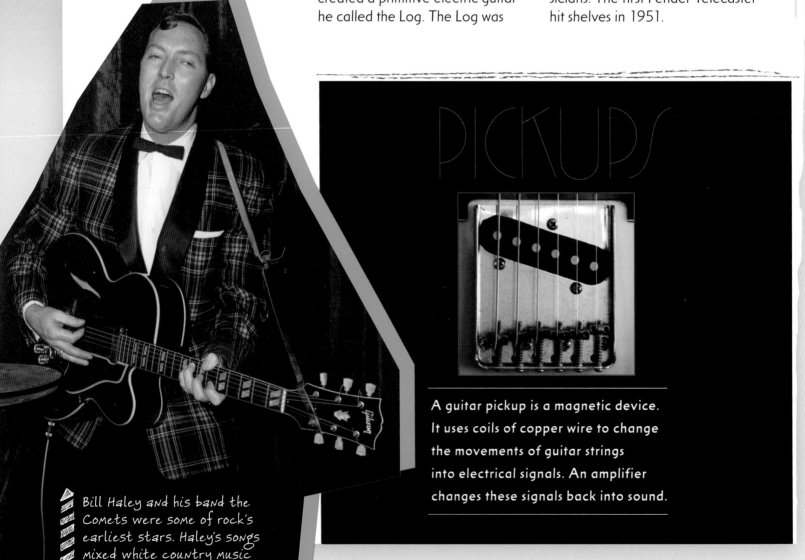

Bill Haley and his band the Comets were some of rock's earliest stars. Haley's songs mixed white country music and African American R & B.

PICKUPS

A guitar pickup is a magnetic device. It uses coils of copper wire to change the movements of guitar strings into electrical signals. An amplifier changes these signals back into sound.

Fender's guitars were built on an assembly line. Each part was the same size from one guitar to the next. If something broke, a musician could easily replace it. The Telecaster's solid design has remained mostly unchanged for more than sixty years.

In 1951 the Gibson Guitar Corporation realized that it needed an electric guitar to compete with the Telecaster. Gibson called its guitar the Les Paul in honor of the inventor of the Log. But the Les Paul guitar looked absolutely nothing

Les Paul was a musician, but he made his biggest impact as an inventor. Paul designed a solid body electric guitar. It was a perfect fit for rock music.

like the Log. It was made from rich mahogany wood and was covered with metallic-gold paint.

The Les Paul had a darker, richer sound than a Fender guitar. The Les Paul was also heavier. The new guitar's heavy body and

JUKEBOXES and the AMERICAN TOP 40

Jukeboxes were the iTunes of the 1950s. For a nickel, a person could play any of the latest songs. A mechanical arm would lift up the record, which spun on a miniature turntable inside of the machine. Every jukebox held up to forty records. So radio stations started doing weekly countdowns of the forty most popular songs in the United States. The American Top 40 list inspired other popular charts, such as *Billboard* magazine's Hot 100 list of popular singles.

"humbucking" pickups soon made the Les Paul a favorite of rock guitarists. It sounded great at high volumes. As bands began to play through bigger and bigger "amps," the Les Paul helped shape the sound of rock.

ROCK 'N' ROLL
RADIO

The disc jockey (DJ) Alan Freed played R & B and rock records on the radio throughout the 1950s. Freed was one of the first DJs to send the sounds of the electric guitar directly into people's homes. He helped expose millions of people to African American musicians such as Chuck Berry. White audiences had never heard Berry's music before.

Before the 1950s, the many styles of music played by African Americans were often lumped together as "race music." Record companies had invented the term race music as a way to label jazz and blues records. The term reflected the racially biased attitudes many whites held at the time. It was first used in an advertisement in 1922. Since many white teenagers avoided "race records," Freed gave this music and others a new name: rock 'n' roll.

Rock 'n' roll may have originally been an urban slang term for sexual activity. But most of Freed's listeners didn't know the earlier meaning. Freed is believed to be the first person who applied the term to music.

The guitarist Chuck Berry was one of rock's pioneers. Berry was a blues musician who played to racially mixed audiences. Some historians believe that rock 'n' roll didn't truly begin until Berry recorded the song "Maybellene" in 1955. With the snappy electric blues of "Maybellene," Berry almost single-handedly invented the sound of rock guitar.

Famous rock guitarists such as Keith Richards of the Rolling Stones started making music after listening to Chuck Berry records. In the late fifties, Berry recorded a series of songs that would become all-time classics, including "Roll over Beethoven" (1956) and "Johnny B. Goode" (1958). Every rock 'n' roll record since then, from the Beatles to the Black Keys, owes a debt to Chuck Berry.

HAIL TO
THE KING

In 1954 a young truck driver wandered into Sun Studio in Memphis, Tennessee. He asked producer (the person who supervises recording) Sam Phillips to help him cut a record. Phillips was skeptical, but eventually he agreed. The young man's name was Elvis Presley.

A few years earlier, Phillips had recorded the original version of "Rocket 88." Phillips also discovered other early rockers such as Jerry Lee Lewis and Roy Orbison. But Sam Phillips's name will forever be associated with Elvis Presley.

Sun Studio recorded twenty-five songs by Presley in 1954. In 1955 Phillips sold Presley's recording contract to the company RCA Victor. RCA released Presley's first album, *Elvis Presley*, in 1956. Five of the album's songs went to No. 1. Presley had more than a dozen Top 40 hits in the space of a single year. He became the King of Rock 'n' Roll.

Elvis Presley played a mixture of gospel, blues, and a form of electric country music called rockabilly. His good looks helped him cross over into movies. His leather-jacket style helped inspire the Beatles' early look. And his songs would soon be covered (played) by hundreds of musicians.

Not everyone was happy about Presley's success. African American musicians had written some of the songs he performed. Presley sold millions of records, but the people who wrote those songs didn't share equally in Elvis's success. The issue of unfair payments would continue in the music business for decades.

Chuck Berry, performing here in 1968, is rock music's original guitar hero. He recorded a series of classic songs throughout the 1950s, including "Maybellene" (1955).

Little Richard became known for his wild stage presence. He put energy into every performance, including this late 1950s show.

"TUTTI-FRUTTI" TIMES TWO

Little Richard was a 1950s suburban parent's nightmare: an African American performer who screamed like the devil and sometimes dressed like a woman onstage. "Little" Richard Penniman's father had kicked him out of their Georgia home at the age of sixteen. After leaving home, Little Richard became one of music's earliest rock stars.

Little Richard knew how to put on a show. He would pound on his piano, shouting and hollering. He'd mimic the sound of the drums with his voice. He'd even roll on the ground.

In 1955 Little Richard cut a record called "Tutti-Frutti." It was the wildest thing many listeners had ever heard. The original lyrics of "Tutti-Frutti" were too explicit for 1950s radio. The song's producer hired another songwriter to change the words. But audiences still weren't prepared for Little Richard.

In those days, African Americans had a hard time getting their music played on the radio. White musicians often recorded new versions of black rock 'n' roll songs. In 1956 the white singer Pat Boone recorded a new version of "Tutti-Frutti." Boone's version was dull compared to Little Richard's original recording. But it sold more copies. Decades later, Little Richard's version got the respect it deserved. In 2010 the U.S. government placed the song in the National Recording Registry. The registry honors songs that are important to American history and culture.

THE QUEEN of ROCKABILLY

Country singer **Wanda Jackson** (LEFT) had been playing music professionally since she was in high school. After touring with **Elvis Presley** in 1955, Jackson became one of the first women to release a rock 'n' roll record. Her rockabilly version of Presley's "Let's Have a Party" was a hit in 1960. Fifty years later, Wanda Jackson was back on the charts with *The Party Ain't Over* (2011). **Jack White** of the White Stripes produced the album. It features fierce new versions of country and rock classics.

[Rock 'n' roll] appeals to the base [lowest] in man [and] brings out animalism and vulgarity.

—Asa Carter, speaking to members of the North Alabama White Citizens' Council, 1956

STOP THE MUSIC!

Rock music became popular just as the civil rights movement in the United States was getting under way. In the 1950s, laws supported racial segregation, the separation of blacks and whites. There were whites-only hotels, buses, bathrooms, and more. Race mixing was illegal. Yet suddenly, millions of white teenagers were listening to black musicians. And rock was spreading around the world.

Segregationists hated rock 'n' roll. Some mistakenly thought that rock music was a scheme to corrupt young minds. Groups calling themselves White Citizens' Councils protested outside rock concerts. They smashed rock records. In some cases, these people had real power. For example, the leader of the White Citizens' Council in Alabama was a man named Asa Carter. Carter worked as a speechwriter for George Wallace, the governor of Alabama. But try as they might, the White Citizens' Councils never put a stop to rock 'n' roll.

THE BRITISH INVASION

As American rock 'n' roll took its lumps from critics, British musicians who had grown up listening to Chuck Berry began playing the music. Soon groups from England were scoring hits in the United States. This became known as the British Invasion of the early 1960s.

The Beatles inspired American artists at every stage of their career. George Harrison, John Lennon, Paul McCartney, and Ringo Starr's early smashes were short, smart pop songs. Throughout the 1960s, the group made albums that were full

Throughout the 1960s, British musicians transformed rock 'n' roll. The Beatles ABOVE made beloved albums such as *Revolver* (1966) that were full of original ideas. The Rolling Stones LEFT combined blues music with swagger, sarcasm, and the dance moves of Mick Jagger FAR LEFT.

of new ideas. As songwriters the Beatles hopped from one musical style to another or combined them.

The Rolling Stones also influenced the sound of American rock music. African American musicians had inspired them too. The Stones named their band after a song by the blues guitarist Muddy Waters. The group started out playing rocking versions of blues classics. They went on to write rock classics of their own, such as "Satisfaction" (1965) and "Jumpin' Jack Flash" (1968). The success of singer Mick Jagger, guitarist Keith Richards, and their bandmates helped make Waters and others like him more popular. Powerful performers such as the Kinks and the Who also proved that rock wasn't just an American thing.

FOLK ROCK

While the Beatles were conquering the airwaves, Robert Zimmerman was changing American rock from within. Zimmerman grew up in Hibbing, Minnesota. In 1961 he moved to New York City's hip Greenwich Village neighborhood. Zimmerman became a folk singer named Bob Dylan. Dylan sang songs on an acoustic guitar in the style of folk artists such as Woody Guthrie.

Dylan was an unlikely star, and not just because of his nasally, scratchy voice. At the start of the

1960s, most musicians relied on professional songwriters for material. But Bob Dylan started composing his own lyrics. Before Dylan, rock stars had stayed away from politics too. However, Dylan sang about racial issues and social injustice. He became the voice of a generation.

In 1963 Dylan performed several protest songs at the March on Washington. The march was the biggest civil rights demonstration that had ever taken place in the United States. Americans of many races protested the laws that mistreated people of color. African American leader Martin Luther King Jr. delivered his famous "I have a dream" speech on that same afternoon.

A Los Angeles, California, group called the Byrds took after both Dylan and the Beatles. The Byrds' first album, *Mr. Tambourine Man* (1965),

Bob Dylan made folk music hip among rock fans. His songs of the 1960s have clever lyrics and strong social messages.

featured electrified versions of many Bob Dylan songs. The Byrds' lead singer, Roger McGuinn, played a twelve-stringed electric guitar. The twelve-string guitar had an especially sparkling sound. With Dylan's words and McGuinn's guitar, the Byrds invented a new style known as folk rock. Later, the Byrds helped create psychedelic rock. They included moody elements of Indian music in their songs. The Byrds' 1966 release "Eight Miles High" is a dreamy, psychedelic classic.

The same summer *Mr. Tambourine Man* arrived, Bob Dylan went electric. Dylan had been scheduled to perform at Rhode Island's Newport Folk Festival. The audience expected him to play a set of acoustic songs. But when Dylan came onstage, he was holding an electric guitar. His fans were outraged! They thought that Dylan had betrayed the folk scene. Looking back, it's hard to see what the fuss was all about. But at the time, electric folk was shocking. Before the decade's end, bands such as Creedence Clearwater Revival would write their own electric protest songs about issues such as the Vietnam War (1957–1975).

BRIAN DON'T SURF

In the early 1960s, surfing was huge. Teenagers watched surfing movies and read surfing magazines. A California band called the Beach Boys caught the wave and recorded several songs about surfing. Most members of the band didn't actually know how to surf. But they knew how to sing catchy melodies with challenging vocal harmonies.

The Beach Boys' chief songwriter, Brian Wilson, believed his band could make true art, as the Beatles did. In 1965 Wilson went into the recording studio. The rest of the band was away on tour, so he started making music by himself. He spent many weeks putting together what he hoped would be the ultimate album. It was called *Pet Sounds* (1966).

Wilson used every trick available in the studio. *Pet Sounds* was a masterpiece. The song "Wouldn't It Be Nice" was bouncy and upbeat,

SURF GUITAR

Inspired by the nearby ocean, a California surfer named **Dick Dale** (Richard Monsour) (RIGHT) started channeling the sounds of the surf through his electric guitar. On songs such as "Miserlou" (1962), **Dick Dale and the Del-Tones** captured the thrill of riding on a wave. Dale used a special effect called artificial reverb to create a wet, echoing guitar sound.

Brian Wilson SECOND FROM RIGHT and the Beach Boys, performing here in 1963, started out making upbeat songs about surfing. With the album **Pet Sounds** (1966), they became respected artists.

yet it showed a new maturity. The somber "God Only Knows" featured swirls of different voices and instrumental sounds. **Pet Sounds** inspired the Beatles to record their landmark album **Sgt. Pepper's Lonely Hearts Club Band** (1967).

PEARL

As a teenager growing up in Port Arthur, Texas, Janis Joplin was a misfit. Her classmates made fun of the way she looked and her love of books. Rather than hanging out with them, Joplin started sneaking out to nightclubs. She learned to sing the blues.

As soon as she was old enough, she moved to San Francisco, California. In 1966 Joplin was invited to try out for a local psychedelic rock band called Big Brother and the Holding Company. She became their new lead singer.

Joplin had a powerful set of pipes. When she sang the blues, audiences were amazed. By 1968 Big Brother and the Holding Company had the top album in the United States, thanks to Joplin's gut-wrenching performance of "Piece of My Heart." In 1969 Joplin left the band to pursue a solo career. She performed in front of five hundred thousand people at the Woodstock Music and Art Fair near White Lake, New York. Woodstock was possibly the most famous concert festival of the 1960s.

Janis Joplin spent years battling an addiction to drugs and alcohol. She died in 1970 at the age of twenty-seven after taking the

Janis Joplin releases her powerful voice during a 1968 concert. She had success both on her own and as a member of Big Brother and the Holding Company.

drug heroin. Her final album, *Pearl* (1971), was released shortly after her death. *Pearl* spent nine weeks at the top of the charts. The song "Me and Bobby McGee" went to No. 1.

JIMI
TAKES OVER

In 1966 a former U.S. Army paratrooper named Jimi Hendrix (Johnny Allen Hendrix) headed to England. Hendrix, a guitar player, got together with bassist Noel Redding and drummer Mitch Mitchell. They formed a band called the Jimi Hendrix Experience.

Jimi Hendrix played guitar like no one else. He played it with his teeth. He played it held behind his head. He made his guitar sound like rockets raining from the sky. And his solos were light-years ahead of everybody else's. In 1967 Hendrix played in front of fifty thousand people at California's Monterey International Pop Festival. During the performance, he doused his guitar with lighter fluid and lit it on fire. The performance wowed the festival audience. Later, Hendrix covered Bob Dylan's "All Along the Watchtower" (1968). He added crackling, unpredictable guitar lines to the song.

Hendrix died in 1970 of drug-related causes. Few other artists have had such a big impact in such a short amount of time. Hendrix helped to usher in an era in which rock musicians played extended jams to show off their musical ability. Rock became louder and much more complex. In addition to three-minute pop songs, fans were listening to entire albums, or double albums. It was the beginning of hard rock. ★

Jimi Hendrix played guitar in a way no one had ever heard before. His solos made fans turn up their speakers and made other guitarists sound old fashioned.

♪ MUST DOWNLOAD Playlist

ELVIS PRESLEY
"Hound Dog" (1956)

LITTLE RICHARD
"Keep A-Knockin'" (1957)

CHUCK BERRY
"Johnny B. Goode" (1958)

WANDA JACKSON
"Let's Have a Party" (1960)

BOB DYLAN
"Masters of War" (1963)

THE BEACH BOYS
"God Only Knows" (1966)

THE BYRDS
"Eight Miles High" (1966)

THE DOORS
"Light My Fire" (1967)

JIMI HENDRIX
"All Along the Watchtower" (1968)

CREEDENCE CLEARWATER REVIVAL
"Fortunate Son" (1969)

CRANK IT Up!

Chapter 2

The British heavy metal band Black Sabbath made pounding rock songs such as "Iron Man" (1970). Many other groups imitated Black Sabbath's gloomy style throughout the 1970s.

HARD ROCK BECAME POPULAR AS THE 1960S WERE DRAWING TO A CLOSE.

Hard rock was a natural next step from the music of Jimi Hendrix and the Rolling Stones. People use the term hard rock to mean loud, guitar-heavy rock with roots in blues music. Guitarists play power chords and blues riffs through giant stacks of amplifiers. Drummers play heavy, thudding beats.

Heavy metal became one of the most popular forms of hard rock. In 1969 the British band Led Zeppelin released its first album.

Led Zeppelin took rock in an epic direction, with songs about Vikings and wizards. Led Zeppelin concerts often lasted for hours. The shows were full of jamming and long solos from guitarist Jimmy Page.

In 1969 the British band Black Sabbath also formed. Before Black Sabbath, such artists as Jimi Hendrix had played hard rock at loud volumes. But Sabbath's music was something else entirely. Guitarist Tony Iommi tuned his guitar strings low for a gloomy, sinister sound.

According to lead singer Ozzy (John) Osbourne, Black Sabbath used to notice crowds of people lining up to see horror movies near the band's rehearsal space. People pay lots of money to see scary movies, Ozzy thought, so why not make scary music? The band started writing songs inspired by horror films. Black Sabbath's creepy style would soon be echoed in the United States.

Led Zeppelin became known for its epic stage shows, such as this 1977 performance. Robert Plant LEFT had a voice that could fill arenas. Jimmy Page RIGHT had a gift for guitar solos that rivaled Jimi Hendrix.

NO MORE MR. NICE GUY

Like Black Sabbath, Alice Cooper (Vincent Furnier) was ahead of his time. Cooper formed a rock band with three high school friends in 1967. He quickly made himself into a rock 'n' roll outlaw. An early press release claimed that the name "Alice Cooper" had come to him while he was communicating with the supernatural. A Ouija board had told Furnier that he was the reincarnation (new form) of a seventeenth-century witch named Alice Cooper. When Furnier performed onstage, he *became* Alice Cooper.

Alice Cooper knew that everybody secretly loves a villain. He decided to play the bad guy. During a performance in 1970, someone threw a live chicken onstage. News reports claimed that Cooper had bitten off the head of the bird. When Cooper denied it, fellow musician Frank Zappa told Cooper to keep that to himself. The legend of Alice Cooper became more interesting than the truth.

Cooper quickly embraced the legend. He appeared onstage in zombie makeup and a straight-jacket, with black circles around his eyes. Alice Cooper concerts were half hard rock, half theater. During songs such as "Black Juju" (1971), henchmen strapped Cooper into an electric chair. Lights flashed, sparks flew, and Cooper thrashed about as if he were actually being electrocuted. Critics called it shock rock. Over the next thirty years, countless bands would copy his routine. Each tried to be more outrageous than the last.

In the 1970s, Alice Cooper shocked audiences with his over-the-top performances.

POWER CHORDS

A power chord is the most basic chord that a person can play on the electric guitar. A guitar chord has between two and six notes. A power chord includes just two notes. When played through a loud amplifier, a power chord sounds heavier than chords that use all six strings. Since the 1960s, power chords have been an essential part of hard rock.

SILVER SUITS AND PLATFORM BOOTS

Glam rock started in England. Glam took Alice Cooper's showmanship and dressed it up with glitter and a feather boa. The members of groups such as T. Rex wore silver space suits and eyeliner.

In the early 1970s, British performer David Bowie made glam rock a true art. Bowie created a character called Ziggy Stardust, a space alien who landed on Earth.

The New York Dolls RIGHT played hard rock and wore lots of makeup. The band was inspired by British glam musicians such as David Bowie BELOW. Other American groups took after the Dolls' style.

Bowie was constantly changing his image and his sound. On one album, he'd play hard rock. On the next, he'd record songs inspired by R & B music. Bowie was also one of the first rock stars to embrace electronic music.

In the United States, glam took a harder turn. At the forefront was Lou Reed. In the late 1960s, Reed had been the singer of the Velvet Underground. The Velvet Underground played rock that was unusually dark. The music sounded primitive, but it covered mature themes. The band never had a radio hit, but it influenced many future alternative groups. Reed's greatest chart success was a glam album, **Transformer** (1972). Produced by David Bowie, **Transformer** included the Top 20 hit "Walk on the Wild Side."

The New York Dolls also adopted a glam rock look. The band appeared in lipstick and red go-go boots. Their noisy sound was borrowed from the Rolling Stones. The group broke up in 1974, but the Dolls had made a lasting impression. Their bad attitude helped to inspire the early punk scene. Hard rockers copied their glam style.

THE BAD BOYS from BOSTON

The Boston, Massachusetts, group **Aerosmith** (ABOVE) helped to define American hard rock in the 1970s. Singer **Steven Tyler** (RIGHT), guitarist **Joe Perry** (LEFT), and their bandmates began playing heavy, bluesy songs in 1970. In 1973 Aerosmith wrote one of rock's first power ballads, "Dream On." During a power ballad, music builds up very slowly toward a guitar solo and a big sing-along chorus. The band slowed down near the end of the seventies due to drug abuse and infighting. But they came back strong. In 1986 Aerosmith performed "Walk This Way," a duet with rappers **Run-D.M.C.**—the first major rock and hip-hop team up.

Most bands start off strong and run out of ideas. But Aerosmith enjoyed more success after its members quit drugs and alcohol. They went on to win four Grammys in the 1990s. In 2008 Aerosmith became the first band to be honored with its own Guitar Hero game.

ROCK 'N' ROLL
SUPERHEROES

The band Kiss took glam rock to a new level in 1973. Inspired by Alice Cooper, Kiss started wearing makeup. Each of its four members adopted a unique character: Starchild (Paul Stanley), Spaceman (Ace Frehley), Catman (Peter Criss), and the Demon (Gene Simmons). No one knew what the members of Kiss actually looked like.

Kiss concerts were massive spectacles. Hundreds of electric lights lit the stage. Gene Simmons would come out dressed in a suit of armor, clutching a bass guitar shaped like a battle-ax, and spitting fire. Despite the band's wild stage shows, early record sales were slow. Then, in 1975, Kiss released its breakthrough record **Alive!** It was a double album, recorded in concert. The roar of the crowd was so intense that Kiss sounded as if

Kiss put on bigger, bolder concerts than the hard rock groups that came before them. The band's members dressed like comic book characters. Their shows featured flames and fake blood.

it were playing in front of twenty thousand people. And pretty soon the band was. Kids lined up to see their real-life superheroes. (The band admitted to using overdubs—parts recorded in a studio—a few decades later.)

Kiss took advantage of the massive spending power of the new Kiss Army. Many of Kiss' biggest fans were still in grade school, the perfect age for lunch boxes, action figures, and even a Kiss Kamping set. The innocence of Kiss's preteen fan base was somewhat at odds with the adult content of Kiss songs such as "Calling Doctor Love" (1977).

The band's record sales started to slump again in the late seventies. In 1983 the remaining members of Kiss decided to "unmask" themselves. The event was front-page news, and the new Kiss found success as a straight-up heavy metal band. But the demon makeup is what Kiss will always be remembered for.

WILD GIRLS

Guitarist Joan Jett (Joan Larkin) was seventeen when she formed the Runaways with a fifteen-year-old drummer named Sandy West. The Runaways' lineup solidified in 1975, with Lita Ford on lead guitar, Jackie Fox on bass, and

Joan Jett was the leader of legendary hard rock band the Runaways. She later had solo success with songs such as "Bad Reputation" (1981).

SISTER ACT

Heart (RIGHT) became one of the biggest groups of the 1970s and the 1980s, thanks to a series of hard-rocking hits, including "Crazy on You" (1976) and "Barracuda" (1977). Guitarist **Nancy Wilson** (RIGHT) and her older sister Ann (LEFT) led the group. Heart's 1975 debut album *Dreamboat Annie* combined chunky guitar riffs with Ann's powerful voice. Critics called the Wilson sisters the female Led Zeppelin. By 1990 Heart had scored more than a dozen Top 40 hits, including "These Dreams" (1985) and "Alone" (1987). The group's 2010 album *Red Velvet Car* put them in the Top 10 once again.

Cherie Currie on lead vocals. Critics treated the Runaways like a novelty act. Few people had seen an all-girl band playing hard rock. And the Runaways were barely old enough to drive! But the band's members played their own instruments and wrote their own songs.

The Runaways released their first album in 1976. It was full of stripped-down guitar sounds. American audiences didn't know what to make of them, but the Japanese treated the Runaways like major rock stars. The group sold more records in Japan than it did in the United States.

The band split up in 1979. Lita Ford went on to record heavy metal albums. Joan Jett launched a new band, the Blackhearts. Twenty-three record companies rejected Jett's new group. So she decided to form her own record label with producer Kenny Laguna. It was a good decision. Joan Jett's second solo album—*I Love Rock N' Roll* (1981)—sold more than ten million copies. The title track was a No. 1 hit for seven weeks.

METAL GOES POP

By the late seventies, heavy metal was getting too serious. Bands were recording concept albums inspired by science fiction and classical music. These concept songs could be twenty minutes long—but they weren't always fun. Van Halen changed all that with its debut album. Led by lightning-fast guitarist Eddie Van Halen, Van Halen played upbeat California beach music with a bright metallic sheen.

The highlight of Van Halen's first record is a one-minute, forty-two-second guitar solo called "Eruption" (1978). Instead of plucking the strings with a guitar pick, Eddie Van Halen tapped them with his fingers, using both hands to hammer on the frets. Rock guitar would never be the same.

Van Halen's singer David Lee Roth was a natural-born showman. Diamond Dave executed high-flying karate kicks during songs. With his long feathered hair and spandex pants, Roth seemed larger than life. There was just one problem: Diamond Dave and Eddie didn't get along. In 1985 Roth left the band. But by that time, the group had already inspired countless acts to merge pop music with metal. New pop-metal bands such as Bon Jovi rose to the top of the charts.

Van Halen rose to fame playing fun hard rock songs that are made to sing along to.

DUDE LOOKS LIKE A LADY

In the 1980s, American heavy metal bands started wearing lipstick. Musicians pulled on tights and teased their hair out until it looked like a lion's mane. Their music became known as glam metal, or hair metal.

Glam metal started in Los Angeles. To get noticed, bands in Los Angeles had to have the right look. This required lots and lots of hair spray. Bands such as Poison and Mötley Crüe posed for photographs wearing thick layers of makeup. Groups placed ads in the back of newspapers with notes like: "New band seeks lead guitarist. MUST HAVE HAIR."

The members of Mötley Crüe became known for their hair metal music—and for their dangerous behavior.

Many musicians in the California glam metal scene consumed dangerous levels of drugs and alcohol. Mötley Crüe was one of the biggest bands in Los Angeles. On December 8, 1984, Mötley Crüe singer Vince Neil got into a head-on collision with another vehicle after he had been drinking. His friend Nicholas Dingley, who was riding in the passenger seat, died almost immediately from injuries he suffered during the crash. Neil avoided prison and continued making music. But the event was one of many signs that the widespread partying had dangerous consequences.

Numerous deaths also occurred in the Los Angeles glam metal scene due to drug overdoses. Nikki Sixx (Frank Feranna Jr.) was one of the lucky ones. Sixx was another member of Mötley Crüe. Sixx overdosed on the illegal drug heroin in 1987. When an ambulance arrived to treat him, Sixx had no pulse (heartbeat). The bassist had been dead for two minutes before medical workers jolted him back to life. Following their troubled 1980s, Neil and Sixx continued to make music and struggled to stay drug and alcohol free.

THE FILTHY FIFTEEN

In 1984 author and activist Tipper Gore gave her daughter Karenna a copy of the album **Purple Rain** (1984). **Purple Rain** was the sound track to a movie starring the R & B artist

Prince. When Karenna started listening to the record, Gore was shocked by its lyrics. Gore, the wife of then U.S. senator Al Gore of Tennessee, wanted the music industry to stop selling R-rated music to children under the age of eighteen.

Gore found an ally in Susan Baker. Baker was the wife of James Baker, then U.S. Secretary of the Treasury. In May of 1985, Gore and Baker formed the Parents Music Resource Center (PMRC). The PMRC wanted to place a rating system on popular music. To draw attention to its cause, the PMRC published a list of fifteen songs unfit for kids and teens. The Filthy Fifteen included Top 40 hits by pop singers Madonna and Cyndi Lauper. But most of the songs on the list were by heavy metal bands, including "We're Not Gonna Take It" by Twisted Sister (1984). The PMRC argued that the song encouraged children to attack their parents.

In September of 1985, members of the U.S. Senate called for public hearings on the content of pop and rock albums. At the hearings, the PMRC blamed metal bands for promoting sexual assault and violence. Its leaders called on music professor Joe Stuessy. Stuessy testified that "heavy metal music [was] categorically different" from other types of music. "Its principal themes are . . . perversion and Satanism [devil worship]," Stuessy argued.

Tipper Gore LEFT and Susan Baker RIGHT formed the Parents Music Resource Center (PMRC) in 1985. The group sought to place a ratings system on music. It criticized the lyrics of heavy metal songs.

> I am married. I have a three-year-old son.
>
> I was born and raised a Christian and I still [stick] to those principles. Believe it or not, I do not smoke, I do not drink, and I do not do drugs.
>
> I do play in and write the songs for a rock and roll band named Twisted Sister
>
> —Dee Snider of Twisted Sister, speaking before the U.S. Senate, 1985

MRS GORE

The PMRC failed to silence groups like Twisted Sister and Van Halen. However, in November of 1985, the Recording Industry Association of America agreed to put a Parental Advisory sticker on albums with explicit lyrics.

ULTIMATE METAL

When James Hetfield and Lars Ulrich met in 1981, they began a partnership that would reshape heavy metal. Ulrich had taken out an ad in the newspaper. He was looking for other musicians who were interested in playing music in the style of British metal groups like Iron Maiden. Hetfield responded. Together with guitarist Dave Mustaine and bassist Cliff Burton, Hetfield and Ulrich set out to create the *ultimate* metal band. They called themselves Metallica.

In 1983 Metallica prepared to record its first album. Mustaine's behavior was out of control due to drinking and drug abuse. So the band recruited Kirk Hammett to be its new lead guitarist. With Hammett on lead, Metallica's songs became more melodic and complex than the metal songs of the 1970s. Hammett had studied classical music. Metallica's songs often included three or four different sections, similar to the movements (sections) of classical symphonies.

Metallica built up a worldwide following among metal fans throughout the 1980s. Burton was killed in a tour bus accident in 1986. Jason Newsted and Robert Trujillo later played bass for the band. When the video for the group's song "Enter Sandman" debuted on the cable channel MTV in 1991, Metallica achieved huge crossover success. The band's album ***Metallica*** (1991) sold more than 15 million copies.

THE LAW OF THE JUNGLE

The hard rockers of Guns N' Roses had been playing in sleazy nightclubs for years before music executive David Geffen saw the group. The band's members dressed in glam metal fashions, but their sound was gritty. Lead guitarist Slash (Saul Hudson) wrote music inspired by the bluesy hard rock of the 1970s. The lyrics of Axl Rose reflected the rough life he had lived on the streets of Los Angeles.

Geffen pressured MTV into playing Guns N' Roses' video for "Welcome to the Jungle" (1987) as a personal favor. MTV aired the video at five in the morning, when

Dee Snider, the lead singer of Twisted Sister, stole the show. Snider noted that Gore had claimed one of his songs, "Under the Blade" (1982), was about sexual assault. "The lyrics she quoted have absolutely nothing to do with these topics," Snider said. "On the contrary, the words in question are about surgery and the fear that it instills in people." Snider had written "Under the Blade" for guitarist Eddie Ojeda, who had to undergo throat surgery.

most viewers were asleep. Almost immediately, the station started getting hundreds of requests to replay the song. The band's album **Appetite for Destruction** (1987) went to No. 1.

Guns N' Roses did not enjoy the long-term success of Aerosmith or Metallica. Throughout the 1990s, several members were fired or quit, including Slash. When a bad mood caused Axl Rose to walk offstage at a 1992 concert with Metallica, fans destroyed parts of the stadium. Fans have also had lukewarm reactions to Rose's attempts to recapture success, such as the decade-in-the-making album **Chinese Democracy** (2008). But **Appetite**'s songs have become rock radio classics. ★

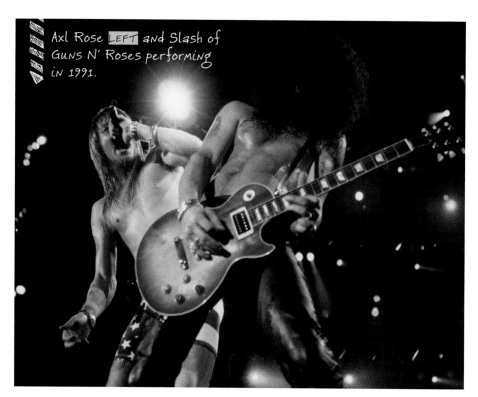

Axl Rose LEFT and Slash of Guns N' Roses performing in 1991.

MUST DOWNLOAD Playlist

ALICE COOPER
"I'm Eighteen" (1970)

LOU REED
"Satellite of Love" (1972)

NEW YORK DOLLS
"Personality Crisis" (1973)

AEROSMITH
"Dream On" (1973)

KISS
"Detroit Rock City" (1976)

HEART
"Barracuda" (1977)

VAN HALEN
"Eruption" (1978)

JOAN JETT
"Bad Reputation" (1981)

MÖTLEY CRÜE
"Shout at the Devil" (1983)

GUNS N' ROSES
"Welcome to the Jungle" (1987)

METALLICA
"One" (1988)

3 WE MAKE OUR Own Rules

Iggy Pop and his band the Stooges were ahead of their time. In the late 1960s, the Stooges started playing music that people would later call punk rock.

JAMES OSTERBERG WAS A PUNK ROCKER BEFORE PUNK EVEN EXISTED.

Osterberg had played in a Detroit, Michigan, band called the Iguanas. His friends nicknamed him Iggy. As Iggy Pop, Osterberg formed a group called the Stooges in 1967.

The Stooges played rock so raw that it sounded like caveman music. Ron Asheton's guitar buzzed like an electric saw. The band became known for its wild live shows. At the 1970 Cincinnati Pop Festival, Iggy stripped off his shirt and waded out into the crowd. He began to crawl over the tops of people's heads. He grabbed a jar of peanut butter and smeared it on his chest. The band played on. At a gig in New York City, Iggy slithered around a stage that was covered with broken glass. At the end of the show, Alice Cooper rushed Iggy to the emergency room. But Iggy just wanted to know if anyone had taken pictures.

The Stooges released their first album in 1969. **The Stooges** was produced by John Cale, a former member of the Velvet Underground. Sales were poor. The Stooges' record label dropped them after their second album also failed to sell. To make matters worse, Iggy started using heroin.

The Ramones played superfast pop songs in tight jeans and leather jackets.

The band nearly collapsed.

In 1971 David Bowie befriended Iggy. Bowie helped Iggy get a new record deal. Iggy put his group back together and asked James Williamson to play lead guitar. Ron Asheton moved to bass.

In 1973 Iggy and the Stooges released **Raw Power**. David Bowie oversaw the recording. Bowie wanted **Raw Power** to sound savage, like someone beating on a log. But something went wrong. The record just sounded muddy and faint. Everyone was disappointed, and the band broke up. Even so, **Raw Power** inspired other bands to play punk

rock—rock that was fast, simple, and loud. In 1977 Iggy celebrated kicking his drug habit with the classic song "Lust for Life."

JOEY IS A PUNK ROCKER

The Ramones formed in 1974 and perfected punk music over the next few years. Lead singer Joey Ramone (Jeffry Hyman) was a shy Jewish kid with a passion for comic

Punk rock became known for its extreme sounds. Punk fans dressed in extreme styles too, such as this fan's spiked hairdo.

books. Joey had met his bandmates while he was growing up in Queens, New York. Guitarist Johnny Ramone (John Cummings), bassist Dee Dee Ramone (Douglas Colvin), and drummer Tommy Ramone (Thomas Erdelyi) filled out the original lineup.

The Ramones weren't very fashionable. With their leather jackets and torn blue jeans, the group looked like rejects from a biker movie. Their music was out of step with what was being played on the radio too. Joey liked pop music from the 1960s. He wanted his group to sound like the Beach Boys. And they did—at warp speed.

On their debut album **Ramones** (1976), the band burns through fourteen songs in twenty-nine minutes. The longest song on the record lasts only two and a half minutes. The Ramones' music was rock stripped down to its simplest parts. There was no time for jams or long solos. Some people argued that the Ramones couldn't play their instruments. But it took skill to perform so many tunes so quickly during concerts.

The band played more than twenty-two thousand concerts during its lifetime. After twenty years of touring and several lineup changes, they finally achieved their first gold record (500,000 copies sold) in 1994: the 1988 best-of collection **Ramones Mania**. In 2011 the Ramones received the Grammys' Lifetime Achievement Award.

PUNK FASHION

Richard Hell (Richard Meyers) (RIGHT) **played in New York City punk bands including Television and the Heartbreakers. With his torn T-shirts, safety pins, and spiky hair, Hell created the look of punk rock in the 1970s. Famous British punk bands such as the Sex Pistols imitated Hell's roughed-up style later in the decade.**

THE CBGB SCENE

The Ramones was one of several bands that played at the New York City club CBGB (Country, Bluegrass, and Blues) in the mid-1970s. CBGB was one of the few places in the city where new bands could perform. It became the birthplace of New York punk.

Although the Ramones played speedy three-chord pop songs, what really defined punk was the freedom to make any sort of noise. The CBGB bands created many kinds of music. Patti Smith was a published poet. She started putting her poetry to music, backed by guitarist Lenny Kaye. By 1975 the Patti Smith Group was playing sold-out shows four times a week at CBGB. Smith became one of the first musicians from the New York punk scene to sign a record deal. Critics praised her debut album *Horses* (1975). The popular arena rocker Bruce Springsteen took note too. He wrote the song "Because the Night" (1978) for Smith to perform.

Singer Deborah Harry and guitarist Chris Stein had been dating when they formed the band Blondie in 1975. Blondie's first releases were punk records. But the band's third album, *Parallel Lines* (1978), included disco (dance) tunes. Some of Blondie's early fans were horrified. Many punks hated disco. Even so, the song "Heart of Glass" became a No. 1 hit.

Groups such as Blondie became known as New Wave bands. New Wave was pop or dance music for people who liked punk's attitude.

Patti Smith, performing here in 1978, was part of the New York punk scene. But her music sounded very different from that of the Ramones. Songs such as "Land" (1975) were ragged and loose yet poetic and thoughtful.

Punk rock started in the United States, but it was very unpopular there in the seventies. Punk had to go to the United Kingdom in order to succeed. In England the snotty punk band the **Sex Pistols** scored a No. 1 album in 1977, despite their controversial single "God Save the Queen" being banned from the radio. Political punks the **Clash** became major rock stars. A couple of years later, British post-punk bands appeared. Groups such as **Gang of Four** and **Joy Division** borrowed drum beats from dance music and mostly ignored rock's blues roots.

In 1976 a group of teenagers in Dublin, Ireland, formed a band called **U2**. They were inspired by punk, but they didn't want to sound like the snarling Sex Pistols. U2's guitarist the **Edge** (Dave Evans) created a chiming, echoing new guitar sound. Singer **Bono** (Paul Hewson) had a voice that was made to fill stadiums—and eventually did.

In Iceland the singer **Björk Guðmundsdóttir** (usually just Björk) (RIGHT) played in punk and post-punk bands throughout the early eighties. In 1986 she helped form a successful Icelandic alternative band called the Sugarcubes. After her time with the **Sugarcubes**, Björk moved to England and began a solo career. Her albums explore many different musical styles.

Deborah Harry of the band Blondie shows off her punk attitude. Blondie broke through to pop and dance audiences with hits including "Heart of Glass" (1978).

Members of the group Bad Brains pose for a picture in the mid-1980s. Bad Brains was one of the first bands to play hardcore punk music.

New Wave bands used electronic keyboards or borrowed from Jamaican reggae music. The B-52's, one popular New Wave group, dressed in 1950s-style clothes and played silly surf-rock songs.

One of the most successful New Wave bands was Talking Heads. Talking Heads made dance music that was artistic and weird. Many of their songs were based on African rhythms. Singer David Byrne delivered songs such as "Psycho Killer" (1977) in a nervous-sounding voice. The band played its first show at

CBGB in 1975, opening for the Ramones. Talking Heads' music became popular on college campuses.

FASTER, TOUGHER, HARDCORE

While New Wave bands were making punk rock that was goofy and danceable, hardcore punk bands went in a more aggressive direction.

Bad Brains of Washington, D.C., was one of the first groups to play hardcore punk. It became one of the most famous African American punk acts. Bad Brains was originally a jazz band. After listening to British punk records, the band started playing rock and reggae at breakneck speeds.

If Bad Brains was the fastest hardcore band, California's Black Flag worked the hardest. Black Flag's sound was tough as nails. So were the members of the band. Hardcore fans liked to "slam dance,"

> In those days, if there wasn't some kind of outbreak or police intervention [at a concert,] then it wasn't all that memorable.

—Henry Rollins (SECOND FROM RIGHT) on his time in Black Flag, 1994

smashing into one another at shows. Oftentimes, the police tried to break up hardcore concerts. Black Flag shows sometimes ended in riots.

Guitarist Greg Ginn formed Black Flag in 1977. The band's most well-known singer, Henry Rollins, joined in 1981. He was muscular and covered in tattoos. He had his nose broken during his first performance, after a man pulled Rollins off the stage and punched him in the face.

Black Flag was one of the first punk bands to go on a nationwide tour. Its members traveled thousands of miles in the back of a van. There were no websites in the 1980s. Black Flag had to book its own shows by calling unfamiliar clubs on the phone. The band earned an average of five dollars per day on tour. In the years following Black Flag's 1986 breakup, Henry Rollins became a Hollywood actor, a published author, and an unlikely TV host.

MARCHING THROUGH GEORGIA

While glam metal bands converged on Los Angeles and New Wave bands made noise out east, the members of R.E.M. were living

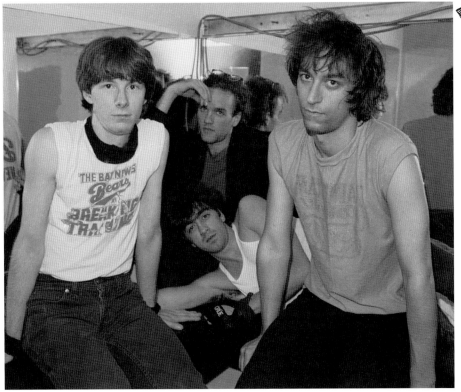

worry about ratings or advertisers, as most stations do.

In 1987 R.E.M. scored its first Top 10 hit with "The One I Love." That same year, Rolling Stone called R.E.M. America's Best Rock and Roll Band. Over the next twenty years, R.E.M. became one of the biggest groups in the world. Spurred on by more hits during the 1990s, the band sold more than 70 million records. In 1996 Warner Bros. offered R.E.M. $80 million to renew its contract. It was the largest record deal in history at that time and proof that college rock could be big business.

in the college town of Athens, Georgia. The group was influenced by Patti Smith's poetic punk and the folk rock of the 1960s. Guitarist Peter Buck sometimes wrote music on old-fashioned instruments such as the mandolin. Instead of following trends, R.E.M. built a fan base with memorable songs such as "It's the End of the World as We Know It" (1987) and "Stand" (1988).

R.E.M. played its first gig in 1980, at a birthday party for drummer Bill Berry's girlfriend. The band later spent months on the road, playing the same grimy clubs as

Black Flag. R.E.M.'s debut album, **Murmur**, was released in 1983. Rolling Stone magazine named it the best record of the year. **Murmur** even beat out Michael Jackson's **Thriller**—the best-selling album of all time.

Despite early praise, R.E.M. had a hard time getting radio play. This is why bands such as R.E.M. were labeled alternative artists. With their unusual sounds, they became an alternative to groups that received more airplay. Their music was usually first heard on college radio stations. The volunteer DJs on college stations got to pick their own music. They didn't have to

A GIGANTIC
INSPIRATION

In 1986 Kim Deal moved to Boston, Massachusetts. Around that time, she spotted an ad in the back of the Boston Phoenix. A group called the Pixies was looking for a bass player. The Pixies wanted someone who was influenced by "Hüsker Dü and Peter, Paul and Mary." Hüsker Dü was a hardcore band. Peter, Paul, and Mary were folksingers

R.E.M. wasn't the only band that college DJs loved to play. **Sonic Youth** (ABOVE) formed in New York City in 1981. The band's guitarists, **Thurston Moore** and **Lee Ranaldo**, invented new ways to tune their guitars. Sometimes they used new tunings for only one song. This approach helped them create guitar sounds no one had heard before.

Minnesota's **Hüsker Dü** played some of the heaviest rock on Earth. Hüsker Dü started as a hardcore punk band. But listeners who got past the noise heard catchy melodies inspired by 1960s pop music. Hüsker Dü had two lead singers, **Grant Hart** and **Bob Mould**. Each singer had his own style of performing. Bob would scream and holler, while Grant had a softer, sweeter voice.

of the 1960s. Deal was intrigued. She was also the only person who showed up for the audition. Soon she was in the band.

The Pixies had a unique style from the start: soft verses, loud choruses. The band switched between pretty melodies and lead singer Charles Thompson's high-pitched shrieks. Guitarist Joey Santiago played fierce, Latin-influenced leads. Pixies lyrics were humorous and sometimes creepy.

In March of 1987, the band recorded a demo tape and sent it to record companies to demonstrate their sound. Meanwhile, Thompson decided to take a stage name: Black Francis. Thompson wanted his name to be something memorable, just like Iggy Pop. The Pixies didn't get offers from sending their demo to American record labels. But the British record label 4AD took a chance on the group.

The Pixies became more popular in England than they were in the United States. Their first release, **Come on Pilgrim** (1987), spent twenty-nine weeks on the British charts. The Pixies went back into the studio to cut the album **Surfer Rosa** (1988). Producer Steve Albini ignored popular fads in music recording. Many producers at the time tried to make drums sound as big and booming as possible. But Albini told drummer David Lovering to set up his drum kit in a restroom. Albini

The Pixies mixed together quirky lyrics, Latin-inspired guitar playing, and the shrieks of singer Black Francis RIGHT.

taped microphones to the floor to capture the room's echoes. The result sounded more natural than most rock of the time.

The Pixies followed **Surfer Rosa** with three more albums. Songs such as "Gigantic" (1988) and "Monkey Gone to Heaven" (1989) became hits with critics. The band broke up in 1993, but its members have sometimes played live together since then. Even before the break-up, other musicians took inspiration from the band's sound. Kurt Cobain of Nirvana would later admit that with "Smells Like Teen Spirit" (1991), he "was basically trying to rip off" the Pixies' soft-loud-soft style. ★

♪ MUST DOWNLOAD *Playlist*

IGGY AND THE STOOGES
"Search and Destroy" (1973)

RAMONES
"Blitzkrieg Bop" (1976)

DEAD BOYS
"Sonic Reducer" (1977)

TALKING HEADS
"Psycho Killer" (1977)

B-52S
"Rock Lobster" (1978)

BLONDIE
"Heart of Glass" (1978)

CARS
"Just What I Needed" (1978)

PATTI SMITH
"Dancing Barefoot" (1979)

HÜSKER DÜ
"Something I Learned Today" (1984)

SONIC YOUTH
"Silver Rocket" (1988)

chapter 4

NIRVANA'S NINETIES: Grunge and More

ON A COLD DAY IN JANUARY OF 1991, THE MEMBERS OF THE WASHINGTON, D.C., PUNK BAND FUGAZI CLIMBED ONTO A STAGE IN THE CITY'S LAFAYETTE PARK.

Fugazi had planned to perform at a rally against homelessness. Then they learned that the United States was about to send troops to Iraq after the country invaded its neighboring country Kuwait. The concert became a protest against the war.

"In D.C., there are thousands of people living on the streets," said singer Ian MacKaye. "It's [unbelievable] that with the billions and billions of dollars that are being spent in the Middle East, that we can't spend more for the people who are dying here!"

Fugazi launched into one of the songs off its album **Repeater** (1990).

MacKaye and Guy Picciotto traded vocals as their guitars created a complicated wall of sound. Joe Lally played slow, jumpy bass lines. Brendan Canty's drumming held it all together.

Fugazi's mixture of punk guitars and funky rhythms made it one of the most influential bands in alternative rock. But Fugazi was as famous for its business practices as it was for its music. Fugazi didn't sell merchandise. The band played all of its concerts in Washington, D.C., for charity. In 1993 Fugazi even

turned down a multimillion dollar contract with Atlantic Records. And MacKaye co-ran a record label, Dischord Records, which was designed to pay artists fairly.

Fugazi's attitude created tension with the mainstream music industry. But the problems the band confronted were very common. Throughout the 1990s, alternative musicians struggled to maintain their integrity, despite the pressure to sell more records.

> " People say 'Why are you marking the twentieth anniversary of your record label?'...
>
> Because for nineteen-and-a-half years people told me that 'It won't work.'
>
> And after twenty, they just have to say 'Well, I guess it did.' "

—Ian MacKaye (left) of Fugazi, 2001

The members of Nirvana, pictured here in 1991, were fans of alternative groups such as Sonic Youth and the Pixies. But unlike those earlier musicians, Dave Grohl LEFT, Kurt Cobain MIDDLE, and Krist Novoselic RIGHT became surprise megastars.

GRUNGE

When punks started listening to Black Sabbath, grunge was the result. Grunge rockers played heavy riffs with punk-rock attitude. The music genre developed in the Pacific Northwest. In the early 1990s, it swept the nation.

Kurt Cobain of the Aberdeen, Washington, band Nirvana became the face of the grunge movement. Cobain took the soft-then-loud sound of the Pixies and wrote even catchier songs. The music video for Nirvana's song "Smells Like Teen Spirit" debuted on MTV in September of 1991. It was an immediate sensation.

When the chorus of "Teen Spirit" kicked in, people found themselves singing along, even though they couldn't make out half of Cobain's words. The music had enough grit to get people rocking but also a memorable pop melody. Glam metal seemed to vanish overnight. By 1992 Nirvana had the No. 1 album in the United States.

SEATTLE
SOUNDS

Nirvana wasn't the only grunge band to wade into the mainstream. The Seattle, Washington, bands Soundgarden and Pearl Jam helped take the music nationwide. Soundgarden sounded like

Perry Farrell (Peretz Bernstein) was the lead singer of a rock band called **Jane's Addiction**. In 1991 Farrell created the Lollapalooza Festival, an alternative music concert tour.

The music onstage during the first Lollapalooza tour was sometimes hard rock, sometimes punk, and sometimes hip-hop. Lollapalooza introduced many people to alternative culture. After seeing the **Red Hot Chili Peppers** (ABOVE) perform, thousands of young people got body piercings or tried "crowd surfing." The Lollapalooza tour no longer takes place. But in 2005 the festival found new life as a series of concerts each year in Chicago.

Led Zeppelin. But its songs were heavier. Lead singer Chris Cornell's powerful vocals grabbed listeners. "Black Hole Sun," from Soundgarden's album *Superunknown* (1994), became a Top 10 hit.

Pearl Jam guitarist Stone Gossard and bassist Jeff Ament had played in the first grunge band in Seattle, Green River. After Green River broke up in 1987, Gossard and Ament tried to form a hair band. That group ended when the band's singer died of a drug overdose. In 1990 the two started jamming with guitarist Mike McCready.

A California surfer named Eddie Vedder heard a tape of Gossard's and Ament's music. Vedder composed lyrics for the songs and visited Seattle to audition. He became the group's singer within a week. The new band, Pearl Jam, released its first album *Ten* in August of 1991. Sales of *Ten* started to pick up a few months later, after Nirvana's first hit. By the end of 1992, Pearl Jam was selling more records than Nirvana.

Some critics said the members of Pearl Jam were posers. They noted Gossard and Ament's glam-metal past. Kurt Cobain accused Pearl Jam of trying to cash in on the success of "Smells Like Teen Spirit." But Pearl Jam turned away from fame. For a time, the band stopped making music videos. They insisted on low concert ticket prices. They played benefits for organizations they cared about.

Pearl Jam was another grunge rock success story. The band took inspiration from the hard rock of the 1970s. Singer Eddie Vedder BOTTOM often sang about social issues.

Kurt Cobain performs at a filmed MTV concert in 1993. By that year, Cobain was struggling with his new fame.

ALL
APOLOGIES

Nirvana's singer, Kurt Cobain, had a hard time dealing with fame. He had suffered from depression for much of his life. He felt uncomfortable with stardom and the lack of privacy that went along with it.

As a teenager, Cobain had been bullied. Once his album *Nevermind* (1991) became a hit, Cobain began to feel that bullies were showing up at his concerts. He was horrified to learn that

FLYING THE FLANNEL

People said that **Kurt Cobain** dressed like a lumberjack. This wasn't a fashion statement. In Aberdeen and elsewhere in the Northwest, people wore flannel to keep warm. But Cobain's T-shirt, blue jeans, and flannel uniform stood out next to glam metal's silk scarves and yellow spandex.

Taking their cue from **Nirvana**, department stores and fashion magazines promoted plaid fabrics and long underwear as grunge fashion. Designer Marc Jacobs even created a line of high fashion grunge inspired clothing. Models walked down the runway dressed in plaid shirts and combat boots. But the members of Nirvana themselves shopped at thrift stores.

Singer Gwen Stefani (ABOVE) **of No Doubt wasn't a part of the Riot Grrrl movement. But No Doubt's song "Just a Girl" (1995) showed a similar attitude. The pop-rock tune criticized unfair treatment of women. No Doubt had been performing in California since 1986, but it wasn't until Stefani began writing songs that the group became famous. The band's third album Tragic Kingdom (1995) was a smash hit. Stefani herself became a fashion icon.**

a couple of men had assaulted a woman while listening to one of his songs. If these people were his fans, Cobain wanted nothing to do with them.

In 1993 Nirvana scored another hit album with *In Utero*. By that time, Cobain was also struggling with his addiction to the illegal drug heroin. As his depression worsened, Cobain used heroin more and more. He had to be rushed to the hospital several times. On April 5, 1994, Kurt Cobain committed suicide. He left behind a young daughter, a wife (Courtney Love of the band Hole), and countless brokenhearted fans.

After Cobain's death, grunge ended almost as quickly as it began. Even so, alternative music had claimed a place on radio and on TV. And Nirvana drummer Dave Grohl found success with a new alternative group, the Foo Fighters. There was no going back.

REBEL GRRRLS

The Riot Grrrl movement got started around the same time Americans discovered grunge. For many young women in the United States, Riot Grrrl was more important. A group of writers and musicians started this feminist (pro-female) punk movement. They formed bands and printed their own zines (small magazines).

Riot Grrrl had no official leaders, but Tobi Vail and Kathleen Hanna were well-known members. Vail and Hanna played in the punk band Bikini Kill. When Bikini Kill played concerts, Hanna would invite all the women in the audience to move toward the front. This created a safe space where women could dance without being pushed around.

Riot Grrrls also organized around political issues. They raised awareness about sexual abuse and promoted sexual health. But the news media often portrayed them as a bunch of silly girls. Tired of the way that journalists wrote about them in magazines such as *Spin* and *Newsweek*, Riot Grrrls declared a media blackout. Many refused to speak to reporters. The movement began to fade in 1994, but its spirit inspired many people. Riot Grrrls Corin Tucker and Carrie Brownstein formed a band called Sleater-Kinney. The band released its first album in 1995. Critics at major magazines began calling them the best rock band in the United States.

POP ROCKS AND WOODSTOCK

Green Day formed in Berkeley, California, in the late 1980s. Guitarist Billie Joe Armstrong, bassist

RAP ROCK and SLACKROCK

Other styles of guitar music developed alongside grunge. **Rage Against the Machine** mixed heavy metal and rap. **Zach de la Rocha** (RIGHT) wrote fierce lyrics about politics and inequality. Guitarist **Tom Morello** supplied some of the 1990s' most memorable guitar riffs.

Beck Hansen, known as **Beck** and the group **Pavement** took after alternative bands like **R.E.M.** They both made alternative music for people who didn't dig grunge's gloominess. Some critics mistook the songwriting styles of Pavement's singer **Stephen Malkmus** and Beck for laziness. These artists often sang nonsense phrases for lyrics. But on a closer listen, their songs ere surprisingly clever.

Green Day kicks off a 2004 concert. The band's humorous, poppy punk music won over audiences in the 1990s.

Mike Dirnt (Mike Pritchard), and drummer Tre Cool (Frank Wright) spent the next few years playing small clubs. On Green Day's first nationwide tour, the punk band printed its own T-shirts. At some of these early concerts, fewer than ten people showed up.

Armstrong had a talent for writing great hooks and catchy melodies. Throughout the early 1990s, the band sold one hundred thousand copies of its first albums through the tiny label Lookout! Records. With better distribution and a proper music video, the possibilities were endless. Compared to its early recordings, Green Day's third album—**Dookie**—had a much smoother sound. **Dookie** came out through Reprise Records, a larger label, in early 1994.

Later that year, Green Day seized their moment. The band was playing in front of 350,000 people at the concert festival Woodstock '94. Rock fans were still upset about the death of Kurt Cobain. Green Day's punk music was the perfect antidote. It was poppy and silly and totally upbeat. Their show quickly turned into a mud fight, which was broadcast on MTV. **Dookie** shot up the charts, selling 15 million copies. In 1995 Green Day became the first punk band to win a Grammy Award.

Along with fellow pop-punk band the Offspring, Green Day brought punk rock out of the gutter and into American malls. The Offspring's 1994 album **Smash** sold over 11 million copies. Other bands soon followed in their footsteps, playing upbeat songs about teen life. The new popularity of punk had some downsides. The shopping mall punk born in the late nineties, including the music of Blink-182, often featured toilet humor in large doses. Groups such as Bikini Kill had inspired young women to form their own bands. But fans of Riot Grrrl's political, pro-female punk would have to turn elsewhere for inspiration.

SELLING OUT?

Kevin Lyman was a concert promoter who had worked on the Lollapalooza Festival. In the mid-1990s, Lyman decided to organize his own alternative tour. The Warped Tour launched in the summer of 1995.

The 1995 Warped Tour featured No Doubt and several other groups. It also showcased extreme sports such as skateboarding. In 1996 Lyman secured Vans Shoes as an official sponsor. The event became known as Vans Warped Tour. Over the next fifteen years, the tour continued to grow. It brought alternative music to thousands of teenagers.

Over time the Vans Warped Tour added dozens of businesses and products as sponsors, including Kia Motors and Monster Energy Drink. Its corporate sponsorship has drawn criticism. Punk rock is supposed to help people think for themselves, some have argued. Does the Warped Tour just encourage people to buy stuff? The answer isn't simple. Warped Tour organizers have also worked to promote recycling and solar power.

Corporate sponsorship in rock isn't new. In 1981 the Rolling Stones allowed a cologne company to sponsor their tour. Recent bands such as My Chemical Romance and Paramore have joined the Honda Civic Tour, paid for by a car company. But some artists and listeners believe that using a song to sell a product cheapens the music. In 1993 Grammy-winning musician Tom Waits sued Levi's Jeans to prevent the company from using one of his songs in a commercial.

Corporate sponsorship no longer has such a bad reputation. Music sales have slowed since the 1990s. Concert tours are the main way many musicians make their living. Faced with rising tour costs, some artists have come to depend on sponsors. Even so, other artists continue to say no thanks. ★

MUST DOWNLOAD Playlist

FUGAZI
"Turnover" (1990)

NIRVANA
"Smells Like Teen Spirit" (1991)

PEARL JAM
"Jeremy" (1991)

RED HOT CHILI PEPPERS
"Under the Bridge" (1991)

PAVEMENT
"Summer Babe (Winter Version)" (1992)

SMASHING PUMPKINS
"Today" (1993)

BECK
"Loser" (1994)

GREEN DAY
"When I Come Around" (1994)

HOLE
"Violet" (1994)

RAGE AGAINST THE MACHINE
"Bulls on Parade" (1996)

SLEATER-KINNEY
"Call the Doctor" (1996)

5 ROCK IN THE New Millennium

Julian Casablancas from the band the Strokes performs in 2006. The Strokes played new songs styled after early punk music.

IN THE LATE 1990S, THE MOST POPULAR FORM OF ROCK MUSIC WAS RAP-ROCK, OR NU METAL.

Rap-rock bands such as Limp Bizkit played snarling, angry songs. Limp Bizkit's singer Fred Durst spoke-sang lyrics over the sound of heavy guitars. Nu metal got a bad reputation after hundreds of fans started a riot and attacked one another during the Woodstock 1999 music festival.

Fans who wanted something else from rock music wouldn't have long to wait. Emo (emotional hardcore) rockers were more willing to show their sensitive side. Their music found a place on the charts and MTV in the early 2000s. A garage rock revival started around the same time. New bands such as the White Stripes and the Strokes took rock 'n' roll back to the basics, looking to Lou Reed and the Rolling Stones for inspiration. Later, bands embraced dance beats or southern sounds. In the new millennium, there was a style of rock for everyone.

GETTING EMOTIONAL

Emo broke wide open in the 2000s. This type of expressive guitar rock started in Washington, D.C., in 1985. The first emo band was a group called Rites of Spring. At the time, violent punk fans known as skinheads were ruining hardcore shows by starting fights. Singer Guy Picciotto and his friends decided to take back the hardcore scene. They played thoughtful, soul-bearing punk. Skinheads hated it. After Rites of Spring broke up, Picciotto and bassist Brendan Canty joined Fugazi.

Bands like Sunny Day Real Estate and the Promise Ring defined emo music in the 1990s. Sunny Day Real Estate moved away from hardcore punk. The band's music could go from softest whispers to deafening roars. Singer Jeremy Enigk sounded as if he was constantly on the verge of tears. The Promise Ring sounded more like a pop band, but it had a do-it-yourself attitude. The group would play at nightclubs in front of hundreds of people or play for dozens of teenagers in a basement. The Promise Ring sold thousands of records just by word of mouth.

Jimmy Eat World was the first emo band to sell more than one million records. The band had been playing basement shows for years. They had signed a contract with a large record company, only to get dropped. Instead of giving up, the band decided to pay for its next album itself. The finished recording, **Bleed American** (2001), included the Top 10 hit "The Middle."

Other emo bands followed in Jimmy Eat World's footsteps. Within a few years, emo music was featured in blockbuster films such as *Spider-Man 2* (2004). Dashboard Confessional showed MTV viewers the emotional power of the acoustic guitar. Fall Out Boy mixed emo with mainstream pop and received a Grammy nomination in 2006. Fall Out Boy later recorded music with hip-hop superstar Kanye West.

NEW YORK COOL

Many rock bands of the 2000s looked to the past while making new music. The singer Julian Casablancas first met guitarist Albert Hammond Jr. at a boarding school in Switzerland. In 1999, back in their hometown of New York City, they formed the Strokes and started writing songs. The music sounded like the early punk bands played at CBGB.

The Strokes recorded their first album **Is This It** (2001) in a basement. The band wanted to capture

By the 2000s, **Green Day** had made it OK for a punk group to get played on the radio or MTV. And by then, teenagers of the 2000s had their own punk-pop superstars. Teen idols such as Canada's **Avril Lavigne** (LEFT) sported punk fashions, while **Good Charlotte** created pitch-perfect, radio-friendly rock songs. For many listeners, punk *was* the new pop.

the feel of a live performance. They didn't want the record to sound "too clean." Each of the tracks was recorded in a single take, with old equipment. Many critics thought **Is This It** to be one of the best albums of the decade.

Around the time the Strokes got their start, other New York bands were making music that sounded like the post-punk and New Wave music of the early 1980s. The Yeah Yeah Yeahs and Interpol played fashionable alternative music fit for dancing. In 2005 a Las Vegas band called the Killers won the MTV Video Music Award for Best New Artist with this dance-punk sound. Five years later, President Barack Obama invited the Killers to perform at the White House.

OUT OF THE
GARAGE

When John (Jack) Gillis started making music, he was fixing sofas in a Detroit upholstery shop. He apprenticed under a man named Brian Muldoon. Muldoon taught White how to repair furniture. He also encouraged White to learn guitar. Together they formed a

Karen O. is the singer for New York rock group the Yeah Yeah Yeahs. This band is known for hits such as the moody love song "Maps" (2004).

Meg White LEFT and Jack White RIGHT of the White Stripes shook up music fans with their raw, bluesy rock. They also confused fans by claiming to be brother and sister. (In fact, they were a divorced couple.)

band called the Upholsterers. They once hid copies of an Upholsterers record inside one hundred pieces of furniture.

In 1996 White married a woman named Meg White. White took his wife's last name. Shortly after they married, Jack and Meg formed a band called the White Stripes. Jack played guitar. Meg kept time with a primal thump. There was no bass player.

The White Stripes were a throwback to the early days of rock 'n' roll. Jack White's guitar playing sounded half like the Stooges and half like Led Zeppelin. But his true love was the blues music of the American South. He borrowed from the music that had inspired early rockers.

The White Stripes drew attention for their style as well as their music. Onstage, Jack and Meg wore three colors: red, black, and white. The band's equipment was in those colors too. Meg's drum kit was painted like a candy cane.

Jack played cheap guitars through crummy amps. The music wasn't always perfect. But it

was a breath of fresh air for many rock fans. Jack and Meg divorced in 2000 but continued playing music together. By 2011 the White Stripes had taken home six Grammy Awards and five MTV Video Music Awards. However, the White Stripes formally split as a band that year.

THE SOUTH RISES

While the Strokes were reviving the sounds of the 1970s, southern rockers Kings of Leon were conquering the airwaves overseas. The Followill brothers (Caleb, Nathan, and Jared) grew up in the suburbs of Nashville, Tennessee. In 1999 they formed Kings of Leon with their cousin Matthew. The group found early success in England, where

audiences embraced the band. Early Kings of Leon records were southern-fried garage rock. Songs such as "Molly's Chambers" (2003) featured fuzzy guitar riffs. On their debut album **Youth and Young Manhood** (2003), the Kings of Leon sounded like the White Stripes' shaggy southern cousins.

Kings of Leon's fourth album, **Only by the Night** (2008), embraced a more polished arena rock sound. It helped the group score hits in its homeland. The song "Use Somebody" was Kings of Leon's most successful recording to date. It won three Grammy Awards, including Record of the Year. Around that time, another family act started making waves. North Carolina siblings Scott and Seth Avett lead the folk rock group the Avett Brothers. The group has won over mainstream fans with albums such as **Emotionalism** (2009).

THE DIGITAL AGE BEGINS

At the turn of the millennium, technology changed rock music. Music fans started downloading songs from the Internet in the form of MP3 sound files. A website called Napster made free sharing and downloading easy. But this type of music sharing, piracy, is illegal. The music industry didn't know what to do. Record stores had been selling compact discs for ten to twenty dollars. But many people jumped at the chance to download the music of a CD for free instead of buying the album.

The members of Metallica were angry that so many people were stealing their recordings. In 2000 Metallica sued Napster. Napster soon filed for bankruptcy. However, record labels still had a major problem. Everyone was starting to listen to music through MP3 files on computers or on new MP3 players. But record companies weren't selling MP3s—just CDs—and so they were losing money on the MP3s that people shared instead of buying the album.

Computer companies such as Apple thought that millions of people would be willing to pay for legal downloads if they were available. So Apple made the music industry an offer it could not refuse: if record labels agreed to make their music available online, Apple would sell electronic versions through the online music store iTunes. iTunes was

GUITAR HERO

The video game Guitar Hero debuted in 2005. Similar games such as Rock Band (2007) followed. Guitar Hero players used a game controller shaped like an electric guitar to play along with famous rock songs. The game allowed people to interact directly with the music. Guitar Hero also introduced a whole new generation to the classic rock of the 1970s. Sales went up whenever bands were featured in Guitar Hero.

the first legal download service to succeed. It changed the way people bought and listened to music.

SHARING ROCK 'N' ROLL

Technology changed the course of rock music again in 2005. That's when YouTube went online. With this new forum for uploading videos, many musicians began using You-Tube to share their music. In 2007 the band OK Go created a home-made music video for its song "A Million Ways." The video was shot in singer Damian Kulash's backyard. It was one of the first homemade music videos to go viral. Fans have watched it more than 9 million times.

Meanwhile, many music fans were creating MP3 blogs—websites on which they wrote about their favorite musicians and shared songs. If alternative bands such as LCD Soundsystem or Canada's Arcade Fire had been around in the 1980s, they might have become stars on college radio. In the 2000s, they became blog favorites.

Because of the Internet, many bands no longer depend on record labels or radio airplay. A musician can record an album in his or her bed-room and upload it onto the Internet. Within hours, people throughout the world could be listening to the songs. If they like what they hear, they can download the music.

In recent times, rock 'n' roll hasn't been as popular as it once was. Hip-hop is the dominant force within the music industry. But fans continue to feel passionately about the music. California's Coachella rock festival draws more than sixty thousand people each year. Groups such as the Black Keys play sold-out shows. Rappers such as Lil Wayne have em-braced rock music as another form of expression. Thanks to the Internet, the entire history of rock is available to any Web user. And kids who grew up playing *Guitar Hero* have started to form bands as teens or young adults. Rock 'n' roll is here to stay. ★

MUST DOWNLOAD *Playlist*

SUNNY DAY REAL ESTATE
"Seven" (1994)

JIMMY EAT WORLD
"The Middle" (2001)

THE STROKES
"Last Nite" (2001)

WHITE STRIPES
"Fell in Love with a Girl" (2001)

LCD SOUNDSYSTEM
"Losing My Edge" (2002)

MOUNTAIN GOATS
"The Best Ever Death Metal Band in Denton" (2002)

YEAH YEAH YEAHS
"Maps" (2003)

GREEN DAY
"Boulevard of Broken Dreams" (2004)

FALL OUT BOY
"Sugar, We're Goin' Down" (2005)

BLACK KEYS
"Lonely Boy" (2011)

GLOSSARY

album: a collection of songs that is released on a single long-playing (LP) record, a single compact disc (CD), or a multiple-MP3 download

alternative rock: rock music that is released through small record labels or that receives limited-to-no play on mainstream radio or TV

amplifier: an electronic device that makes the sounds of a guitar, bass, or other instrument louder

blues: a form of African American folk music with sorrowful lyrics

corporate sponsorship: the giving of money by a business to an artist, usually in exchange for advertising opportunities

disco: a style of dance music popular in nightclubs in the 1970s that included strings, repeated rhythms, and electronic sounds

glam: a musical style from the 1970s known for its performers' manner of dress, which includes flamboyant makeup and clothing choices

grunge: a musical style from the 1990s in which artists mix elements of punk rock and heavy metal

hardcore: a form of punk rock that is especially fast and aggressive

harmony: the combination of two or more different musical tones at the same moment in a way that is pleasing to the ear

heavy metal: a musical style that started in the late 1960s and is known for its dark themes, fast pace, and gloomy sound. Heavy metal sometimes shows a classical music influence.

New Wave: a musical style from the late 1970s that mixes the attitude of punk with pop melodies or dance sounds

producer: a person who manages a record's recording process. The producer often creates the final mix, adjusting the levels of sound in a song.

psychedelic: a musical style from the 1960s known for its dreamy sounds and use of Indian or Middle Eastern instruments

punk: a musical style from the 1970s known for short, loud, simple-to-play songs

R & B: rhythm and blues is a form of music that originated in the middle of the twentieth century. R & B borrows from African American blues and gospel music traditions.

record label: a company that pays for musicians to record music and then distributes, advertises, and profits from that music

reggae: a type of native Jamaican music. Many punk and New Wave bands were inspired by reggae.

riff: a short series of notes or chords repeated throughout a song, often on guitar

solo: a musical piece within a group performance that spotlights the talents of one person

TIMELINE

1951: Bill Haley and his band record "Rocket 88," perhaps the first rock 'n' roll song.

1955: Chuck Berry releases "Maybellene," which goes on to sell more than one million copies.

1956: Elvis Presley appears on *The Ed Sullivan Show*, a popular television program.

1964: The Beatles appear on American television, kicking off the British Invasion.

1965: Bob Dylan goes electric at the Newport Folk Festival. He helps create a style of music known as folk rock.

1967: Jimi Hendrix goes wild at the Monterey International Pop Festival in California.

1969: The Woodstock Music and Art Fair in New York offers fans three days of peace and music. Artists such as Janis Joplin and the Grateful Dead play.

1973: Aerosmith writes one of rock's first power ballads, "Dream On."

1976: The Ramones release their self-titled first album. The album inspires other bands to play punk music.

1978: Blondie's hit song "Heart of Glass" ushers in New Wave music.

1980: R.E.M. plays its first gig, a birthday party held at St. Mary's Episcopal Church in Athens, Georgia.

1981: Joan Jett releases the hugely successful *I Love Rock N' Roll* after being turned away by numerous record labels.

1987: The video for Guns N' Roses' "Welcome to the Jungle" debuts on MTV.

1991: The first Lollapalooza Festival brings alternative rock to twenty cities.

1994: Nirvana's Kurt Cobain commits suicide, following struggles with depression and drug addiction.

2000: The members of Metallica participate in a lawsuit against the file-sharing site Napster.

2005: The video game *Guitar Hero* is released, renewing interest in classic rock. The game allows rock fans to play along with famous rock songs.

2010: A stage musical based on Green Day's album *American Idiot* (2004) hits Broadway in New York City.

2011: R.E.M. breaks up after thirty-one years. Sonic Youth also disbands after thirty-years.

2012: The Foo Fighters sweep the rock categories at the Grammy Awards, winning Best Rock Song, "Walk," Best Rock Album (*Wasting Light*), and other honors.

MINI BIOS

Bill Haley and His Comets: Bill Haley's band was the first rock group to have a No. 1 hit. Their 1954 recording of "Rock Around the Clock" was featured in the movie *Blackboard Jungle* (1955). The song sold over 25 million copies.

Chuck Berry (born 1926): Chuck Berry was born in Saint Louis, Missouri. He is known for his blues-inspired but original style of guitar playing. In the 1950s, he released a series of songs that helped shape the sound of rock guitar.

Creedence Clearwater Revival: Singer John Fogerty led this San Francisco band. CCR lived in California, but they wrote songs with a swampy, southern feel. The band's song "Fortunate Son" (1969) protested the Vietnam War.

Guns N' Roses: GnR, a Los Angeles hard rock band, formed in 1985. The band rose to fame on the strength of its debut album *Appetite for Destruction* (1987). Drug abuse and infighting caused the band to break up. Singer Axl Rose spent fifteen years and $13 million recording GnR's comeback album *Chinese Democracy* (2008), which features an entirely new band.

Jimi Hendrix (942–1970): Jimi Hendrix was born Johnny Allen Hendrix in Seattle, Washington. In 1966 he moved to England and formed the Jimi Hendrix Experience. The group blew away rock fans when Hendrix returned to the United States, thanks to his guitar playing on songs such as "Purple Haze" (1967).

Joan Jett (born 1958): Joan Jett was born in Wynnewood, Pennsylvania. She helped found the all-girl hard rock band the Runaways in California in the mid-1970s. She also had success as a rock solo artist, releasing albums such as *Bad Reputation* (1982).

Kiss: Kiss is a hard rock band best known for its elaborate stage show and costumes. Each member of Kiss created his own character. Kiss was one of the biggest bands of the 1970s.

Red Hot Chili Peppers: The Chili Peppers are a funk-metal band that rose to superstardom with the release of their fifth album, *Blood Sugar Sex Magik* (1991). The band's bassist, Flea, is considered one of the best bass players in the world.

Patti Smith (born 1946): Patti Smith is a poet and once led the New York City punk band the Patti Smith Group. Smith rose to fame as part of New York's CBGB scene. Critics have praised her powerful, creative lyrics.

Sonic Youth: Sonic Youth was an alternative rock band formed in 1981. The group was famous for its use of unusual guitar tunings. Guitarists Thurston Moore and Lee Ranaldo often shoved drumsticks or screwdrivers between their guitar strings to alter the tone.

Bruce Springsteen (born 1949): Bruce Springsteen is a singer, songwriter, and guitarist from New Jersey. Springsteen gained fans with his songs about working-class life. He has filled arenas for decades with the E Street Band.

Velvet Underground: Singer-guitarist Lou Reed helped form the Velvet Underground in 1964. The group caught the attention of the artist Andy Warhol, who became their manager. The Velvet Underground's sound was intentionally simple and sometimes incredibly loud.

White Stripes: The White Stripes was a two-piece band from Detroit, Michigan, led by the former husband-and-wife team of Jack White and Meg White. The White Stripes played bluesy hard rock using cheap guitars and old-fashioned recording equipment.

▸ ROCK MUST-HAVES

Must-Have Albums

Elvis Presley, *Elvis Presley* (1956)

Beach Boys, *Pet Sounds* (1966)

Jimi Hendrix Experience, *Are You Experienced?* (1967)

Velvet Underground, *The Velvet Underground & Nico* (1967)

Patti Smith, *Horses* (1975)

Ramones, *Ramones* (1976)

Iggy Pop, *Lust for Life* (1977)

X, *Los Angeles* (1980)

Violent Femmes, *Violent Femmes* (1983)

Replacements, *Let It Be* (1984)

Hüsker Dü, *New Day Rising* (1985)

Guns N' Roses, *Appetite for Destruction* (1987)

Pixies, *Doolittle* (1989)

Fugazi, *13 Songs* (1990)

Sonic Youth, *Goo* (1990)

Red Hot Chili Peppers, *Blood Sugar Sex Magik* (1991)

Nirvana, *MTV Unplugged in New York* (1994)

Elliott Smith, *XO* (1998)

Strokes, *Is This It* (2001)

Killers, *Hot Fuss* (2004)

Sleater-Kinney, *The Woods* (2005)

Cat Power, *The Greatest* (2006)

Hold Steady, *Stay Positive* (2008)

Decemberists, *The Hazards of Love* (2009)

Black Keys, *El Camino* (2011)

Must-Have Songs

Chuck Berry, "Maybellene" (1955)

Little Richard, "Tutti-Frutti" (1955)

Dick Dale and His Del-Tones, "Miserlou" (1962)

Booker T. and the M.G.'s: "Green Onions" (1962)

Bob Dylan, "Like a Rolling Stone" (1965)

Big Brother and the Holding Company, "Piece of My Heart" (1968)

Iggy and the Stooges, "Search and De-stroy" (1973)

Aerosmith, "Dream On" (1973)

Kiss, "Black Diamond (Live)" (1975)

The Runaways, "Cherry Bomb" (1976)

Blondie: "Hanging on the Telephone" (1978)

The B-52's, "Rock Lobster" (1978)

Minor Threat, "Filler" (1981)

Joan Jett and the Blackhearts, "I Love Rock 'n' Roll" (1982)

R.E.M., "Swan Swan H" (1986)

Nirvana, "Smells like Teen Spirit" (1991)

Soul Asylum, "Runaway Train" (1993)

Soundgarden, "Black Hole Sun" (1994)

Rancid, "Roots Radical" (1995)

Beck, "Devil's Haircut" (1996)

Modest Mouse, "Cowboy Dan" (1997)

Neutral Milk Hotel, "Two Headed Boy Part 2" (1998)

The White Stripes, "Fell in Love with a Girl" (2002)

Green Day, "Holiday" (2003)

Dropkick Murphys, "I'm Shipping Up to Boston" (2005)

Wild Flag, "Future Crimes" (2011)

⫸ MAJOR AWARDS

American Music Awards (AMA): The AMA ceremony is broadcast each year on the ABC television network. TV host Dick Clark created the AMAs in 1973. Unlike the Grammy Awards, the AMAs are awarded based on polls of the public. In 2011 the AMA for Favorite Artist (Alternative Rock Music) went to the Foo Fighters.

Billboard Music Awards (BMA): The BMAs are awarded by *Billboard* magazine, which tracks the sales of popular music. BMA winners are determined by the sales tracked on the *Billboard* charts. The California band Train took home the BMA for Top Rock Artist in 2011.

Grammy Awards: The Grammys are prestigious music awards given by the National Academy of Recording Arts and Sciences. The Beatles were the first rock band to be awarded the Grammy for Album of the Year, in 1968. Canadian alternative band Arcade Fire made history in 2011 when its album *The Suburbs* won the Grammy for Album of the Year, beating out Lady Gaga and Eminem.

MTV Video Music Awards (VMA): The VMAs have been held every year since 1984. Recent winners of the VMA for Best Rock Video include 30 Seconds to Mars in 2010 and Foo Fighters in 2011.

Rock and Roll Hall of Fame: The Rock and Roll Hall of Fame is a nonprofit organization that inducts, or honors, artists who have made contributions to rock music. Rock fans can visit the Rock and Roll Hall of Fame and Museum in Cleveland, Ohio, to see many pieces of rock history in person. Alice Cooper was among the people inducted to the Hall of Fame in 2011.

⫸ SOURCE NOTES

8 Chris Smith, *101 Albums That Changed Popular Music*, rev. ed. (2007; repr., New York: Oxford University Press, 2009), 6.

8 Ibid., 6.

10 Stephen Holden, "Ooh! My Soul," *New York Times*, October 14, 1984.

11 Linda Martin and Kerry Segrave, *Anti-Rock: The Opposition to Rock and Roll*, rev. ed. (1988; repr., Cambridge, MA: De Capo Press, 1993), 41.

11 Asa Carter in "White Council vs. Rock and Roll," *Newsweek* 47, no. 32 (April 23, 1956), quoted in Linda Martin and Kerry Segrave, *Anti-Rock: The Opposition to Rock and Roll*, rev. ed. (1988; repr., Cambridge, MA: De Capo Press, 1993), 41.

19 Gabriella, "Ozzy Osbourne: The Godfather of Metal," *nyrock.com*, June 2002, http://www.nyrock.com/interviews/2002/ozzy_int.asp (August 21, 2011).

20 Rolling Stone, "Alice Cooper," *rollingstone.com*, n.d., http://www.rollingstone.com/music/artists/alice-cooper/biography (August 21, 2011).

20 Alice Cooper, "Alice Cooper—in His Own Words," *superseventies.com*, n.d., http://www.super-seventies.com/ssalicecooper.html (August 21, 2011).

20 Barbara Mikkelson and David P. Mikkelson, "Dead Puppies," *snopes.com*, May 15, 2007, http://www.snopes.com/music/artists/marilyn2.asp, (August 21, 2011).

25 Steve Huey, "The Runaways: Biography," *Allmusic.com*, n.d., http://www.allmusic.com/artist/the-runaways-p5321/biography (January 2, 2012).

25 Blackheart Records, "Biography," *joanjett.com*, n.d., http://www.joanjett.com/ (January 2, 2012).

26 Kyle Anderson, "Vince Neil Crashes His Car, Kills Razzle Dingley: Wake-Up Video," *newsroom.mtv.com*, December 8, 2010, http://newsroom.mtv.com/2010/12/08/vince-neil-razzle-dingley-crash/ (August 21, 2011).

26 Jon Wiederhorn, "Nikki Sixx Book Covers Girls, Girls, Girls and Drugs, Drugs, Drugs," mtv.com, http://www.mtv.com/news/articles/1470347/nikki-sixx-release-journals.jhtml (August 21, 2011).

27 U.S. Government Printing Office, "Record Labeling Hearing Before the Committee on Commerce, Science, and Transportation, United States Senate, Ninety-Ninth Congress, First Session on Contents of Music and the Lyrics of Records," September 19, 1985, 14.

27 Ibid., 117.

28 Ibid., 73.

27 Ibid., 73.

31 Erik Hedegaard, "Iggy's Trail of Destruction," iggypop.org, November 19, 2003, http://www.iggypop.org/iggypopinterviews2001.html (August 23, 2011).

31 Contactmusic.com, "Iggy & the Stooges Raw Power" Documentary (The Bowie Mix) Video," contactmusic.com, 2010, http://www.contactmusic.com/videos.nsf/stream/iggy-the-stooges-raw-power-documentary-the-bowie-mix (August 23, 2011).

32 RIAA, "Searchable Database," riaa.com, n.d., http://www.riaa.com/goldandplatinumdata.php?content_selector=gold-platinum-searchable-database (August 23, 2011).

36 Paula O'Keefe, "Henry Rollins at 50—Henry Rollins' Big Birthday Party," doom-magazine.com, February 19, 2011, http://doom-magazine.com/doom/henry-rollins-birthday-party-2399 (August 23, 2011).

36 Michael Azzerad, Our Band Could Be Your Life: Scenes from the American Rock Underground 1981–1991 (Boston: Little, Brown, and Company, 2001), 41.

37 Rock and Roll Hall of Fame, "R.E.M. Biography," rockhall.com, n.d., http://rockhall.com/inductees/rem/bio/ (August 23, 2011).

37 Josh Frank and Caryn Ganz, Fool the World: The Oral History of a Band Called the Pixies (New York: St. Martin's Griffin, 2006), 17.

38 Ibid., 70.

39 David Fricke, "Success Doesn't Suck: Rolling Stone's 1994 Kurt Cobain Cover Story," rollingstone.com, January 27, 2011, http://www.rollingstone.com/music/news/kurt-cobain-rolling-stones-1994-cover-story-20110127, (August 23, 2011).

36 Henry Rollins. Get in the Van (Los Angeles: 2.13.61, 1994), 9.

41 Mark Andersen and Mark Jenkins, Dance of Days Two Decades of Punk in the Nation's Capital (New York: Soft Skull Press, 2001), 301–302.

44 Everett True, Nirvana: The Biography (Cambridge, MA: Da Capo Press), 318, 335.

46 Kurdt (sic) Cobain, "Insesticide Liner Notes," completenirvana.co.uk, n.d., http://www.completenirvana.co.uk/php/information/liner.php (August 23, 2011).

45–46 Ibid.

48 Gillian Gaar, Green Day: Rebels with a Cause (New York: Omnibus Press, 2007), 40.

48 Ibid., 63.

49 Daniel Sinker, "Extreme Exploitation: The Selling of the Vans Warped Tour," Punk Planet, November–December 1999, 72–83.

49 Vans Warped Tour, "Sponsors," vanswarpedtour.com, n.d., http://vanswarpedtour.com/sponsors (August 23, 2011).

49 Vince Neilstein, "Exclusive Earth Day Interview: Warped Tour–Rock Star Mayhem Fest Founder Kevin Lyman on His Tour's Green Initiatives," metalsucks.net, April 22, 2011, http://www.metalsucks.net/2011/04/22/exclusive-earth-day-interview-warped-tour-rockstar-mayhem-fest-founder-kevin-lyman-on-his-tours-green-initiatives/ (August 23, 2011).

41 Erik Farseth, Wipe Away My Eyes: A History—Underground Culture and Politics, 1979–1999 (Minneapolis: Abandoned House Books, 2001), 51.

45 Rick Marin, "Grunge: A Success Story," New York Times, November 15, 1992.

51 Andy Greenwald, Nothing Feels Good: Punk Rock, Teenagers, and Emo (New York: Saint Martin's Griffin, 2003), 122–124.

51 Ibid., 104.

52 Martin Roach, This Is It: The First Biography of the Strokes (New York: Omnibus Press, 2003), 68.

52 Ibid., 71.

52 Believer, "Jack White [Musician]: Your Furniture's Not Dead," believermag.com, May 2003, http://www.believermag.com/issues/200305/?read=interview_white (August 23, 2011).

54 Bob Boilen, Jack White, and Robin Hilton, "The Flipside with Jack White: Upholstery and His Rarest Records," npr.org, March 14, 2011, http://www.npr.org/blogs/allsongs/2011/03/14/134458863/the-flipside-with-jack-white-upholstery-and-his-rarest-records (August 23, 2011).

//// SELECTED BIBLIOGRAPHY

Andersen, Mark, and Mark Jenkins. *Dance of Days: Two Decades of Punk in the Nation's Capital.* New York: Akashic Books, 2009.

Azzerad, Michael. *Our Band Could Be Your Life: Scenes from the American Rock Underground 1981–1991.* Boston: Little, Brown, 2001.

Frank, Josh, and Caryn Ganz. *Fool the World: The Oral History of a Band Called Pixies.* New York: St. Martin's Griffin, 2006.

Gaar, Gillian. *She's a Rebel: The History of Women in Rock & Roll.* New York: Seal Press, 2007.

Greenwald, Andy. *Nothing Feels Good: Punk Rock, Teenagers, and Emo.* New York: St. Martin's Griffin, 2003.

Greer, Jim. *R.E.M.: Behind the Mask.* Boston: Little, Brown, 1992.

loudQUIETloud: A Film about the Pixies. DVD. Directed by Steven Cantor and Matthew Galkin. Produced by Jonathan Furmanski, Matthew Galkin, Steven Cantor, Caroline Stevens, and Daniel Laikind. New York: Mvd Visual, 2006.

Smith, Chris. *101 Albums That Changed Popular Music.* 2007. Reprint. New York: Oxford University Press, 2009.

True, Everett. *Nirvana: The Biography.* Cambridge, MA: Da Capo Press, 2007.

Zwickel, Jonathan. "A Ramshackle Errand: The Oral History of the First Lollapalooza." *Spin.* June 2011, 78–86.

//// FURTHER READING, WEBSITES, AND FILMS

AllMusic
http://allmusic.com
AllMusic is the most extensive music website on the Internet, with thousands of entries on rock albums, songs, and artists.

Doeden, Matt. *Green Day: Keeping Their Edge.* Minneapolis: Lerner Publications Company, 2007.
This book follows Green Day from the band's early years in California to the worldwide success it enjoyed later on. Learn about the group's successes and failures on its way to rock stardom.

Gaar, Gillian G. *The Rough Guide to Nirvana.* New York: Rough Guides, 2009.
This illustrated guide to the band Nirvana features color photos, musician interviews, reviews of every Nirvana release, and more. Discover the history behind this talented and sometimes misunderstood rock band.

It Might Get Loud. DVD. Directed by David Guggenheim. Produced by Thomas Tull, David Guggenheim, Lesley Chilcott, Peter Afterman, and Jimmy Page. Steel Curtain Pictures, 2008.
This documentary follows the careers of three rock guitarists: Jack White (White Stripes), the Edge (U2), and Jimmy Page (Led Zeppelin). White, Page, and the Edge also get together and talk about their music.

No Direction Home. DVD. Directed by Martin Scorsese. Produced by Susan Lacy, Jeff Rosen, Martin Scorsese, Nigel Sinclair, and Anthony Wall. Paramount Pictures, 2005.
Director Martin Scorsese edited this documentary from hours and hours of historical footage and interviews. The film traces the life and music of Bob Dylan throughout the 1960s.

Poole, Rebecca. *Jimi Hendrix.* Minneapolis: Lerner Publications Company, 2006.
This biography traces the life of Jimi Hendrix from his childhood to his time in the armed forces to his years of rock superstardom. Find out more about what inspired this guitar legend.

Roberts, Jeremy. *The Beatles: Music Revolutionaries.* Minneapolis: Twenty-First Century Books, 2011.
Find out more about the British group that inspired countless American rock musicians. This book looks at the lives of the Beatles' members before, during, and after their time in rock's most famous group.

Rock and Roll Hall of Fame and Museum
http://rockhall.com/
The official website of the Rock and Roll Hall of Fame features more information about rock music's past. The site also gives visitors a peek at exhibits at the museum and provides profiles of every Hall of Fame inductee.

Sinker, Daniel, ed. *We Owe You Nothing: Expanded Edition.* New York: Akashic Books, 2007.
This book collects interviews with famous punk figures from the award-winning magazine *Punk Planet.* Read the stories behind the music from members of Fugazi, Sonic Youth, Black Flag, and more.

INDEX

ABOUT THE AUTHOR

Erik Farseth holds an MA in journalism from the University of Iowa. His writing has previously appeared in *Punk Planet*, the *Daily Iowan*, *Downtown Journal*, and *Maximumrocknroll*.

PHOTO ACKNOWLEDGMENTS

The images in this book are used with the permission of: © Will Ireland/Metal Hammer Magazine via Getty Images, p. 1; © Dorling Kindersley/Getty Images, p. 2; © Photodisc/Getty Images, p. 3; © Frank Driggs Collection/Archive Photos/Getty Images, pp. 4, 10; © Michael Ochs Archives/Getty Images, pp. 5, 7 (top), 9, 11, 13, 14, 16, 20, 21 (both); © Topical Press Agency/Hulton Archive/Getty Images, p. 6 (left); © Joseph Clark/The Image Bank/Getty Images, p. 6 (right); © Joseph Scherschel/Time & Life Pictures/Getty Images, p. 7 (bottom); Canadian Press via AP Images, p. 12 (left); © Bettmann/CORBIS, p. 12 (right); © Sunset Boulevard/CORBIS, p. 15; © David Redfern/Redferns/Getty Images, p. 17; © Jorgen Angel/Redferns/Getty Images, p. 18; © Richard E. Aaron/Redferns/Getty Images, pp. 19, 25, 37; © Robert Knight Archive/Redferns/Getty Images, p. 22; © Gijsbert Hanekroot/Redferns/Getty Images, p. 23; © Adrian Boot/Photoshot/Hulton Archive/Getty Images, p. 24 (top); © Ron Galella/WireImage/Getty Images, p. 24 (bottom); © Ebet Roberts/Redferns/Getty Images, pp. 26, 38; AP Photo/Lana Harris, p. 27; © Hulton Archive/Archive Photos/Getty Images, p. 28; © Ke.Mazur/WireImage/Getty Images, p. 29; © Ed Perlstein/Redferns/Getty Images, p. 30; © Michael Ochs Archives/CORBIS, p. 31; AP Photo/Greg Wahl-Stephens, p. 32 (top); © Roberta Bayley/Redferns/Getty Images, p. 32 (bottom); © Howard Barlow/Redferns/Getty Images, p. 33; © Marc Grimwade/WireImage/Getty Images, p. 34; © Kevin Cummins/Getty Images, p. 35 (left); © David Corio/Redferns/Getty Images, p. 35 (right); © Erica Echenberg/Redferns/Getty Images, p. 36; © Steve Pyke/Getty Images, p. 39; © Naki/Redferns/Getty Images, p. 41; © Paul Bergen/Redferns/Getty Images, pp. 42, 44; © Henry Diltz/CORBIS, p. 43; © Frank Micelotta/Hulton Archive/Getty Images, p. 45; © Michael Tran/FilmMagic/Getty Images, pp. 46, 52 (top); © Kevin Winter/Getty Images, p. 47; AP Photo/Robert E. Klein, p. 48; AP Photo/Jeff Christensen, p. 50; © Graham Denholm/WireImage/Getty Images, p. 52 (bottom); © Mark Allan/WireImage/Getty Images, p. 53; © Joyce Naltchayan/AFP/Getty Images, p. 54.

Front cover: © Emmanuel Faure/The Image Bank/Getty Images.

Main body text set in Arta Std Book 12/14
Typeface provided by International Typeface Corp